The Memorial Walks

Simon Pope

film and video umbrella

Contents

6   The Memorial Walks
Steven Bode

20   Paintings

26   Walk 1
Recalled by Rex Hancy

30   Walk 2
Recalled by George Szirtes

34   Walk 3
Recalled by Marjorie Allthorpe-Guyton

38   Walk 4
Recalled by Amanda Hopkinson

42   Walk 5
Recalled by Tom McCarthy

46   Walk 6
Recalled by Hari Kunzru

50   Walk 7
Recalled by Nicci Gerrard and Sean French

56   Walk 8
Recalled by Brian Dillon

60   Walk 9
Recalled by Ken Worpole

64   Walk 10
Recalled by Trezza Azzopardi

68   Walk 11
Recalled by Geoff Dyer

72   Walk 12
Recalled by Sally O'Reilly

76   Walk 13
Recalled by Stuart Jeffries

80   Walk 14
Recalled by David Matless

84   Walk 15
Recalled by Iain Sinclair

90   Walk 16
Recalled by Sharon Morris

94   Walk 17
Recalled by Susanna Paisley

101   Sebald Memorial Walk
Recalled by Simon Pope
accompanied by Nicholas Thornton

106   Biographies

The Memorial Walks

Over the course of 2007, starting out before the first leaves began appearing on the trees and only ending after they were turning for autumn, artist Simon Pope made a series of seventeen walks in the company of seventeen different writers. These shared excursions, conducted, in fair weather and foul, across the flatlands and fenlands of East Anglia, were undertaken as part of a unique arts project called *The Memorial Walks*, for which this publication is both an adjunct and a memento. Continuing a long line of artists' (and writers') journeys through both actual and imaginative terrain, *The Memorial Walks*, as its title implies, tied its experience of the landscape to a series of exercises in memory. Before embarking on their respective walks, each of the participating writers (poets and novelists, geographers and travel writers, naturalists and ecologists) was given a different scene from a landscape painting to memorise, and 'carry' with them out into the open country where they would be required to recount it, in as much detail as they could muster, at a particular point en route. A test of their powers

of recall as much as their powers of description, these writers' recollections formed the core of a project which continued to proliferate from its original starting-point: into the gallery, over the internet, and, by highlighting walks that its audience might want to emulate, back into the landscape from whence it came.

These multiple forays into deepest Lincolnshire and Norfolk, extensively documented and photographed, and with each writer's recollection recorded for posterity as a short audio file, followed on the heels of an earlier walk, carried out in the dying days of 2006. An artist who had already attracted considerable attention for a body of work in which a commitment to long-distance walking was allied to a more obviously conceptual preoccupation with the phenomenon of re-enactment and the representation of memory, Pope was one of the first names that Film and Video Umbrella had sought to include in a large-scale exhibition, to be staged in Norwich and Lincoln, that drew much of its inspiration from the writings of the novelist W.G. Sebald, whose digressive literary journeys (often through his adopted home of the east of England) and penchant for vivid yet elegiac observation had struck a chord with a growing number of contemporary artists. Whereas other contributors to the exhibition, entitled *Waterlog*, produced film, video or photographic works that traced familiar Sebaldian motifs or re-visited people or places first encountered in his magnum opus *The Rings of Saturn*, Pope homed in, unsurprisingly, on Sebald's solitary trudges through Suffolk and Norfolk, and the extent to which the repetitive activity of walking functioned as a spur to memory and reflection. Finding common ground also in Sebald's frequent visits to local museums, Pope extended his interest

in the landscape paintings of the Norwich School (Britain's first provincial art movement), whose signature works, by John Sell Cotman, John Crome, James Stark and others, are on permanent display at Norwich Castle Museum and Art Gallery (the launch venue for *Waterlog*). Intrigued by the extent to which Sebald's books are regularly embellished with personal/archival images (including facsimiles of paintings or other historical artefacts), Pope found himself returning, time and again, to one of the closing chapters of *The Rings of Saturn*, which laments the steady disappearance of trees from the East Anglian landscape, and which culminates, particularly hauntingly, in a faded photograph of a row of pines that were decimated by the hurricane of 1987. With this image indelibly planted in his mind, Pope then resolved, on 14 December 2006, the fifth anniversary of the car crash that had claimed Sebald's life, to walk the short distance out of Norwich towards places that Sebald would have known well and where his spirit is, in a sense, most alive. Once there, in memoriam, as if laying down a wreath of words, he would try and recall as much as he could of the trees in the photograph, as a mark of respect. In the depths of a season where absence and loss are most keenly felt, his gesture takes on the added poignancy of being performed in the teeth of a gale, every third or fourth syllable of the recording being lost to the wind.

A hesitant preliminary step in what soon would become a much larger undertaking, this first memorial walk nevertheless suggested an outline for others to follow. After a period of further research in the Norwich Castle archives, in which he was introduced to the many other Norwich School landscapes that were no longer on display to the public, Pope started to consider how these

lesser-known paintings, for all the efforts to cata-
logue and preserve them, were fast disappearing
from memory. As if to restore some of the close
attention they had lacked in their time locked
away in the storeroom, in an attempt to clear the
layers of actual or metaphorical dust that had
accumulated around them, Pope identified ten
such works from the collection that he would ask
well-known writers to hold in their minds; with
each image, and its recollection, to be showcased
on a weekly basis over the two-and-a-half-month
run of the *Waterlog* show. Once this choice had
been made, Pope, myself and my colleagues at
Film and Video Umbrella set out to compile a
shortlist of people, from different walks of literary
life, who it would be interesting to involve in the
project. This early wish-list was weighted towards
writers with a connection to the locality (the poet
George Szirtes, crime fiction authors Nicci
Gerrard and Sean French, the art critic and Norwich
Castle Museum alumnus Marjorie Allthorpe-
Guyton, naturalist Rex Hancy, author of *Notable
Trees of Norwich*, as well as the critic and translator
Amanda Hopkinson, who succeeded Sebald as
the Head of The Centre for Literary Translation
at the University of East Anglia) but later branched
out to include other equally resonant choices,
such as ecologist-activist Ken Worpole, and the
writer and artist Tom McCarthy, whose recent
cult novel *Remainder* was a study in re-enactment
of quixotic, almost operatic proportions. Matched
to one of the available paintings, but with no great
advance information about it, or, indeed, of the
route of the walk they would take with Pope, each
writer, after being greeted at the gallery, was left
alone with their appointed work, albeit with the
instruction to concentrate specifically on a tree
(or trees) at the centre of the scene; to detach it,
almost uproot it, from the painting, and its wider

art-historical context, and simply describe it, or embody it, in its detail and its simplicity, for someone who hadn't seen it, so that they too could then picture it in the same way.

Entrusted to the agency of others, yet equally clearly directed by the hand of the artist, this surrogate, almost scattershot approach is both endearingly arbitrary and part of a larger unfolding design. Nowhere is this shaping influence more evident than in the manifestation of the project in the gallery. Laid out in orderly rows as an integral part of the *Waterlog* show, the ten paintings were grouped together as a series, with priority given to the canvas that was the subject of that week's featured walk. It would be more accurate to say that that particular painting was the only one on public view, since its nine companions were completely shrouded in folds of black silk: a reminder perhaps of the hitherto mothballed invisibility of the image itself, but also an allusion to the ritual practice of covering paintings, or mirrors, in a house where a death had occurred. Pope's injunction generated a minor frisson of controversy among several gallery-goers, who complained that a picture (which would otherwise have been out of circulation anyway) was deliberately, even willfully, withheld from view, and who, ignoring their normal reluctance to tamper with a work of art, often lifted the veil to see what lay beneath. Other visitors wondered why the writer's audio recollection of the painting, confined to a listening post elsewhere in the gallery, or downloadable from the internet, was not in more direct proximity to the scene it described. Keen to exploit this tension between the image and its ghostly echo, Pope persisted with this method of display, deploying the same set-up in the venue in Lincoln to which *Waterlog* travelled later that year, in which

a further seven paintings, drawn from local collections, were recounted by an equally distinguished line-up of authors such as Iain Sinclair, Sharon Morris and Geoff Dyer.

Pared back to this essential core, always adhering to the same strict formal template, the seventeen writers' recollections, each of them centred on their individual adopted trees, also resemble their wider subjects in the way in which an apparently narrow and confining *genus* does not preclude an underlying diversity. Appearing as extracts over the following pages of this publication, but available in full on the project website (www. waterlog.fvu.co.uk), the edited highlights of these larger transcriptions, along with the equally brief snapshots from the walks themselves, nonetheless offer a unmistakable index of the project's scope and complexity. As one would expect, given their facility and sensitivity for language, the participants are both formidably fluent and exceptionally considered in their choice of words. Starting out from an ingrained, professional obligation towards accurate, almost pinpoint depiction, several of the contributors go on to imbue the process of the recall with a considerable degree of nuance and self-reflexivity. Never unnecessarily florid, many of the writers are especially alert to the myriad interplay of form and content, aware that the images they are endeavouring to capture might not only be conveyed in words but also in the ramifying patterns of sentence structure, or in the material unravelling of parallel, yet interdependent, strands of thought. If the spread of human knowledge is traditionally likened to the growth of a tree, it is no surprise when these little stabs at elucidation repeat the analogy in miniature form.

I
John Middleton (1827–1856)
A Fine Day in February, (Hellesdon)
Oil on millboard
Norwich Castle Museum & Art Gallery

Sharing little of the conceptual sleight-of-hand by which another artist famously conjured an oak tree from a set of step-by-step manoeuvres, *The Memorial Walks*, in its feeling for landscape, its emphasis on memory, its ambition to renew, and, at the end of the road, its embrace of fallibility, radiates a refreshing and appealing humanity. At one level, an abstruse and fanciful attempt to replenish the company of trees in a landscape now largely denuded of their presence, it is also a compelling reminder of a fundamental human imperative to both summon up and commemorate what has gone. Conceived in memoriam to Sebald, and played out in the shadow of a storm that, exactly twenty years before, had dealt another devastating blow to some of the last remaining woods and copses in East Anglia, *The Memorial Walks* is, despite this doleful backdrop, a beguilingly uplifting work – testimony to the power (and, of course, the limits) of the written and the spoken word, and their enduring ability to keep the past alive.

Steven Bode

2
John Crome (1768–1821)
Grove Scene
Oil on canvas
Norwich Castle Museum &
Art Gallery

3
John Sell Cotman (1782–1842)
The Silent Stream, Normandy
Oil on canvas
Norwich Castle Museum &
Art Gallery

4
Henry Bright (1810–1873)
Grove Scene
Oil on canvas
Norwich Castle Museum &
Art Gallery

5
Samuel James Sillet
(1764–1840)
The Winfarthing Oak
Oil on canvas
Norwich Castle Museum &
Art Gallery

6
Alfred Priest (1810–1850)
*Beech Trees, Grazing Cattle
to Right*
Oil on millboard
Norwich Castle Museum &
Art Gallery

7
John Berney Ladbrooke
(1803–1879)
The Great Oak
Oil on canvas
Norwich Castle Museum &
Art Gallery

8
James Stark (1794–1859)
Marlborough Forest
Oil on canvas
Norwich Castle Museum &
Art Gallery

9
Samuel David Colkett
(1806/7–1863)
*Landscape with cows in a pool
by a clump of trees*
Oil on oak panel
Norwich Castle Museum &
Art Gallery

10
Joseph Paul (1804–1887)
Poringland Oak
Oil on canvas
Norwich Castle Museum &
Art Gallery

11
Frederick Mackenzie
(1787–1854)
Monks Lane, Lincoln
Watercolour and pencil on paper
The Collection, Art &
Archaeology in Lincolnshire

12
Jean Henri De-Coene
(1798–1866)
Landscape
Oil on panel
The Collection, Art &
Archaeology in Lincolnshire

13
Jean Henri De-Coene
(1798–1866)
River Scene with Men in a Boat
Oil on panel
The Collection, Art &
Archaeology in Lincolnshire

14
Nicholas Van Schoor
(1666–1726)
Landscape with Tree
Oil on canvas
The Collection, Art &
Archaeology in Lincolnshire

15
artist unknown
*Landscape with Buildings,
Cows and Sheep*
Oil on panel
The Collection, Art &
Archaeology in Lincolnshire

16
Alfred George Webster
(1852–1916)
*Mr Bland's Orchard,
Heighington, Lincoln*
Oil on canvas
The Collection, Art &
Archaeology in Lincolnshire

17
Robert Noble (1857–1917)
On the Dean, East Linton
Oil on canvas
The Collection, Art &
Archaeology in Lincolnshire

Drayton

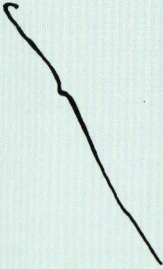

River Wensum Valley

Walk 1
Drayton to the River Wensum Valley
25 January 2007

John Middleton (1827–1856)
A Fine Day in February, (Hellesdon)

Recalled by Rex Hancy

Rex Hancy:

"… The sun has come through and it's beginning to lighten the landscape. There's not a leaf on any of the trees yet. And those trees are nearly all willow trees. They're growing on the edge of the river. And one or two little watery channels, I don't know whether they're meant to be drainage ditches or just feeder streams, or what they are, but they are actually picked out by the trees standing by the side. Most of the trees have been pollarded…"

[…]

"One of the most significant trees is standing beside at a slightly drunken angle, so it feels inclined to be horizontal rather than perpendicular, but I'm sure those roots will dig in deeper, because the top is obviously taken off at very, very frequent intervals…"

"[The trees] are growing more densely than you would expect to see in the more open landscape and surely they have been deliberately cultivated to give a little bit of break from the wind. Most of them are branching out into many, many shoots, which really ought to be coppiced, again to keep the tree going, because if you carry on that work you are pretty well immortalising the tree. While people are taking that step every generation, the tree outlasts everybody."

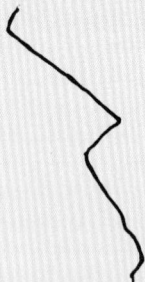

Upton

Upton Marshes

Walk 2
Upton to Upton Marshes
26 January 2007

John Crome (1768–1821)
Grove Scene

Recalled by George Szirtes

George Szirtes:

"…What you have is a great bank of trees on one side of the picture. In this case, it's on the right. They've got quite white barks. The light is very diffuse. It's catching in the clouds, which are banking up in the far distance. These trees snake away to the left of the picture into a patch of darkness…"

[…]

"The other thing you notice is that a number of the trees have been cut down. I was trying to tell whether the trees have been cut down with an axe or with a saw, because they look very smooth at the bottom. Either the trees were being used for something or they were old and dying trees. In fact, not all the trees look as though they are in their first spring of youth. Some may be dying. In fact, the most dramatic part of the painting is the foreground tree on the right. There are whole lot of exposed and lit branches, writhing and twisting this way and that. It's quite a loud tree visually and it reaches up into the sky..."

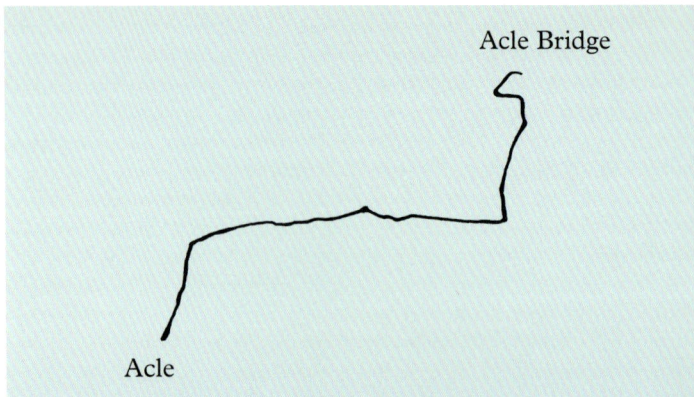

Walk 3
Acle to Acle Bridge via Hermitage Marshes
2 February 2007

John Sell Cotman (1782–1842)
The Silent Stream, Normandy

Recalled by Marjorie Allthorpe-Guyton

Marjorie Allthorpe-Guyton:

"The trees are fat and billowing and the colour
is molten gold and silver and greys and greens.
And the whole mood of the picture… It's called
The Silent Stream and you can understand why,
because the stillness is there in the painting:
the water, the reflections; everything is a frozen
moment. You have these heaps of trees; there are
several trees on the left. The composition is very
weighted toward the centre and the left. And then,
the stillness of those reflected in water below and
to the right."

[…]

"The heavier clumps of trees are probably
grouped around patches of water. It need not be
a stream at all; it could simply have been a muddy
pool. It could easily have been something around
a marl pit. The trees blot out the sky, so the trees
are completely the theme, the main theme, the
whole essence of the picture…"

South Walsham Broad

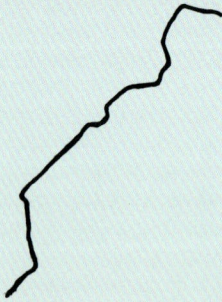

South Walsham

South Walsham Broad
6 February 2007

Henry Bright (1810–1873)
Grove Scene

Recalled by Amanda Hopkinson

Amanda Hopkinson:

"There is one large tree that is foregrounded, just behind the water and then a row of smaller ones, a glade or a grove, going off to the right as you look at it. And beside the larger tree is its fallen pair. There is one that looks as though it's blasted and come down in a storm, maybe after a flash of lightning. But it's already been semi-sawn up, for logging, perhaps for furniture-making rather than burning because it's a solid tree like an oak or an elm. And over in the background there's a kind of bifurcated view: off to the left as you look at the image there are more trees receding into the distance and there are hints of other things. The picture's quite dark on this side. There's a figure walking into the distance but it can also be read as more and more trees..."

Walk 5
Acle to Acle Bridge
22 February 2007

Samuel James Sillet (1764–1840)
The Winfarthing Oak

Recalled by Tom McCarthy

Tom McCarthy:

"I remember a very large oak tree that's been cleft in twain, maybe by a storm, or maybe it's just grown that way. It's got two parts and they coil around each other, like the double-helix coil of a DNA pattern. And on the right, there's this half coiling upwards that's really dead; it's completely derelict and ruined. On the left, there is another half of trunk which is also dead but it's got a new trunk emerging out of it which is very alive; it's very fecund, and it's blossoming and it's got a whole canopy of green and lots of smaller branches and skeins networking against the sky. The derelict part on the right is full of holes; it's like a sort of ruined cathedral, a derelict building. The part on the left, the main trunk, is also hollowed out but it forms a tube – you get the sense that sound would resonate inside it… Even though it's dead it seems like it's quite resonant and would generate some sort of sound, whereas the bit on the right is absolutely desolate, and vandalised. What's interesting, also, about the part of the tree that's the failed part, the really dead part, that part that's cast away like the dead wood of rejected memory, or whatever, what's interesting about it is that it's still there – it hasn't been completely cut-off and destroyed. It's still there, like a ghost, like a material ghost. Like some sort of living-dead reproach that clings to the living part and won't ever be got rid of…"

[…]

"I don't know if that tree ever actually existed, it seems so perfectly symbolic of history, or memory, or trauma."

Cantley

Reedham

Walk 6

Cantley to Reedham
23 February 2007

Alfred Priest (1810–1850)
Beech Trees, Grazing Cattle to Right

Recalled by Hari Kunzru

Hari Kunzru:

"What I can remember seeing is a group of three trees… To the left, nearest to me, is a quite magnificent tree which rises up in a very straight vertical line, and then a branch comes off to the right in the shape of a bow. But it's still a very fat, fat, branch. And opposing it on the left hand side, coming out at two right angles…that's right…there are two major branches coming off to the left of the main trunk, one above the other. And it all disappears into quite murky darkness of spidery dark leaves. It's a very silvery tree. I don't know the name of this tree, because I don't live in a place with trees… There seem to be grey slabs of bark that have peeled away in places, with much more white, or silver wood exposed underneath. But it doesn't look like a birch, or anything like that. It looks like an traditional English tree…"

Haddiscoe

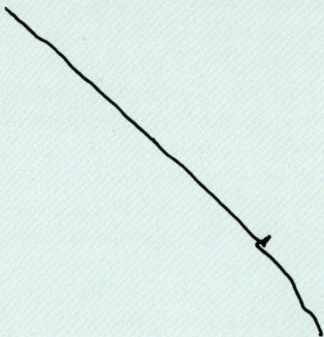

Reedham Ferry

Walk 7

Haddiscoe towards Reedham Ferry
28 February 2007

John Berney Ladbrooke (1803–1879)
The Great Oak

Recalled by Nicci Gerrard and Sean French

Nicci Gerrard and Sean French:

Sean: "As far as I can remember, in the foreground there are two large oak trees. The one on the left has a double trunk…"

Nicci: "…and the one on the left is also lit by the light, so it looks silver and pale green and gold and its bark is also silver and very runnelled…"

Sean: "…and it's got things on it; it may have acorns on it, blotches dotted across it."

Nicci: "…so we think it's sometime in the autumn, and the one on the right, which has much darker green foliage, has a look of end-of-summer greenness about it, and there are a few tinges of gold on the edges."

Sean: "The tree on the left is looking a bit on the fringes, looking not only old, but also bits of it are dying away; branches that are virtually dead, with no foliage on them at all."

Nicci: "…indeed, by the side of the tree on the left there is a dead sapling; a tree that started to grow and then died. And on the right of the greener tree, there's a log…"

Sean: "A tree trunk!"

Nicci: "So there is this sense of these old trees and dead trees beside them, and in the distance, in the clearing, there's a young sapling on the right. So there's this sense of new trees and old trees and dead trees. And the two big oak trees are standing like two pillars at the entrance of what's clearly a managed woodland; they're almost like the gateways to this woodland…"

Sean: "In the very foreground it's as if there are bushy kind of oaks that are hardly growing at all: a kind of blur of green leaves right at the front – there's this oak forest behind, but you just can't make out the details of it, you can just see the shadowy trunks behind. [...] On the far right, going off into the distance, there's this one little thing that breaks the horizon, and then when you go further to the right there's a much more vague, more distant oak; rather wispy oak woodland..."

Nicci: "Clearly a young copse."

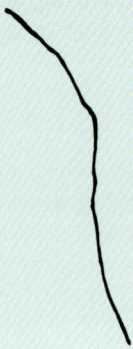

Thorpe St. Andrew

Postwick Marshes

**Thorpe St. Andrew to Postwick Marshes
3 March 2007**

James Stark (1794–1859)
Marlborough Forest

Recalled by Brian Dillon

Brian Dillon:

"The main thing that strikes you first of all is what I think is an oak, on the left-hand side in the foreground. It reminded me immediately of the phrase 'a blasted oak', which I guess means an oak struck by lightning, although it may not have been struck by lightning, because there's a suggestion that it's actually been slightly uprooted; you can vaguely see around the roots that it's leaning towards the right. There's still some foliage on the dead tree, so there's the suggestion that it's still somehow alive. It frames, along with two trees to its right, a kind of archway… I think the trees other than the dead tree…one seems to me to be an oak, the other could well be an elm, or possibly an ash, and it's surrounded by a few, what I believe are called 'suckers', smaller offshoots of the main tree. Those three frame a little arch… On the left-hand side, it's kind of unclear, but it may be a continuation of some more oaks, and there's a sense that you might be at the edge of a much wider expanse of woodland…"

[…]

"Trying to recall it, I just keep coming back to the main, dead tree. And the more I try to picture that, the more it seems actually to dominate a good deal more of the painting that you think at first glance just because there are branches that curve and twist into directions that you don't really see. So in fact the large tree covers…as I recall it, a good fifth of the surface of the painting. It actually snakes over, well over, towards the other two trees and towards the large elm in the middle of the painting, so that it actually, if I think about it now, seems to form the arch that dominates the whole composition."

Rockland Marsh

Walk 9
on Rockland Marsh
23 March 2007

Samuel David Colkett (1806/7–1863)
Landscape with cows in a pool by a clump of trees

Recalled by Ken Worpole

Ken Worpole:

"The first thing that I remembered about that painting was, of course, that there were fences in it. There was a copse of trees, ashes and oaks, that were growing wild, outside of the fences. They were still part of nature, rather than part of the culture, the agricultural farmland of the area. And also they hadn't been coppiced or in any way treated as industrial products. They were part of nature and they were quite magnificent..."

[...]

"So that copse, at the centre of the picture, stands for me as something very strong and resistant to the forces that are happening around it. A copse is a kind of meeting place for trees...a group of trees can have an identity, and represent a form of natural congregation; a natural presence in a landscape where human activity is less important."

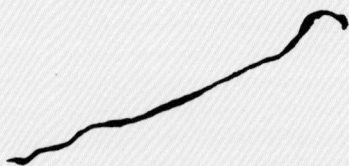

Upton Staithe

Walk 10
on Upton Staithe
3 April 2007

Joseph Paul (1804–1887)
Poringland Oak

Recalled by Trezza Azzopardi

Trezza Azzopardi:

"It was such a massive tree, judging by the tiny people at the foreground of the landscape, that I thought that maybe I should look at it from below. So if I was going to be imagining this tree, I would have to be looking right up into the sky… That doesn't give you any idea of the size or anything, except that if you imagine that you are standing up and have to look right up into the clouds, then that's probably how big that oak tree would be. Which makes me think it probably wasn't that big in real life… And now I think perhaps it wasn't very beautiful, either; because it was a mass, a sort of mass, of what looked like a section of brain. From a distance, it did look as though somebody had just cut a piece of brain, cross-sectioned, and all of those fibres inside were visible. It doesn't make it sound like an attractive oak, as we imagine oak trees to be: this beautiful part of the English landscape. The picture is dominated by this massive oak tree in the right foreground; and in the background there are smaller trees… But the detail of the branches is quite difficult, because the colours look wrong to me: the colours look brown, yellow and orange, and I didn't think there was a great deal of individual detail in the branches…"

[…]

"Out of the top of the oak tree are two great white masses of cloud on either side… So it would appear that the shape of the cloud is echoing the tree."

Potterhanworth Booths

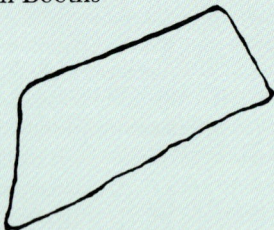

Walk 11
on Potterhanworth Booths
30 July 2007

Frederick Mackenzie (1787–1854)
Monks Lane, Lincoln

Recalled by Geoff Dyer

Geoff Dyer:

"…Whereas somebody who was more at one with the natural world might be able to tell you, might be able to *see* a particular kind of tree, all I'm seeing is this thing called 'a tree'. A tree with very brown leaves. There's a sense that this picture takes place both at the end of a day, towards the end of the day, and towards the end of the season; it's got this doubly autumnal quality because the tree is still fully in-leaf, but it's all turning very, very brown."

[…]

"On the other side, we've got what looks to me like a different kind of tree. The tree on the left, the leaves are coming right the way down to the floor, whereas here we've got the, er…the main bit of the tree which is quite bare of leaves, and then the canopy is less dense than the trees on the other side. But I think what's quite interesting is that they meet and frame the sky, and the cathedral, forming, almost like a Norman arch. I think it's quite common when people are in the forest they talk about the 'cathedral of trees'. So you've got this pun going on: you've got the cathedral in the background being framed by this cathedral of trees…"

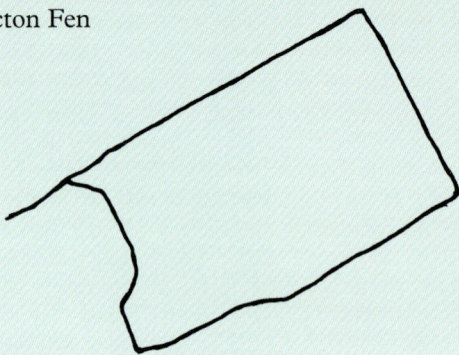

Nocton Fen

Walk 12
on Nocton Fen
31 July 2007

Jean Henri De-Coene (1798–1866)
Landscape

Recalled by Sally O'Reilly

Sally O'Reilly:

"…The main tree is to the left of the right-hand side, and it curves towards the left and then goes back in at the top, to the right… And that main tree has something like a twenty degree angle; the sub-branches that come out, they come out to the left, somewhere near the extreme curve of the tree, they come out on the horizontal and one goes up and one goes down… It has a silvery trunk. I wouldn't hazard a guess at what…to my father's horror, I couldn't identify it. I could say birch. In the left third of the painting, there are two trees in the near-middle distance, and their trunks are painted more hazily, and yet the leaves are not… There's something very friendly, and almost jolly about the tree."

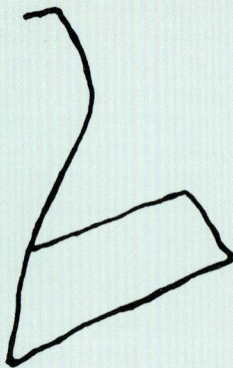

Nocton Fen

Walk 13
on Nocton Fen
22 **August** 2007

Jean Henri De-Coene (1798–1866)
River Scene with Men in a Boat

Recalled by Stuart Jeffries

Stuart Jeffries:

"The first thing to note is that I am completely unsure of what kind of tree the main tree in the foreground is… Behind it is another tree, so there are two trees in the foreground and they are both very closely linked together: their branches seem to be interwoven. And then behind them, there is another stand of trees, almost like a row of trees extending alongside this riverbank… There are very few branches in the first half of the tree's ascent into the sky; there are lots of branches going off to the left of the tree. The tree seems dead or dying towards the bottom of it and flourishes wildly, really wildly towards the top. It seems to be early summer or late spring: the leaves are quite new. And they are all on the outskirts, on the tips of the branches. There's very little in-filling. It's not a solid sea of green at all, as you might expect from an oak, or something. Instead, there are quite bare branches and on the end these new, newish leaves. But the other thing that's utterly striking, tremendously striking, from the start is how there are these bands, on the trunk at the beginning, at the base of the trunk, there are bands of silver, and then black. Silver. Black. The black looks like the tree's been charred, maybe it's deceased in some way, I am not sure… I wonder what sort of tree it is. I've no idea! I should know…"

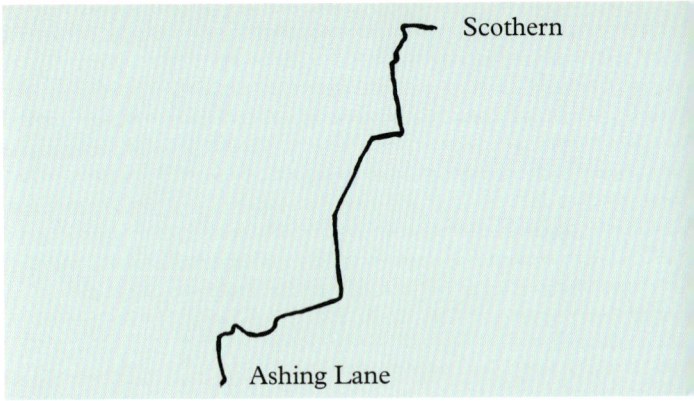

Scothern

Ashing Lane

Walk 14

Scothern to Ashing Lane
14 September 2007

Nicholas Van Schoor (1666–1726)
Landscape with Tree

Recalled by David Matless

David Matless:

"…The tree is twisted, probably of the same species as trees immediately behind it, although I wouldn't begin to try to identify them. As it twists up slightly to the left, the setting sun is catching some light along the left-hand side of it. While initially it looks like a grey blank form, if you look closely at it you can see there's a vividness on the left-hand side where the sun is catching it, and to the left of that dead tree the scene shows a slight opening into a brighter part of the landscape where the sun is still full-on, as it is on the right-hand side…The dead tree is in front of evidently more alive trees – again, which are catching the sun on their backs. They are deliberately set against the sky so you are noticing the particular shade of sunset behind them. It seems that some of the leaves on these trees are turning brown, so perhaps we are going into autumn, or perhaps some of the branches on the trees are themselves not that healthy, so maybe there is a story about decay in apparently healthy and lively trees…"

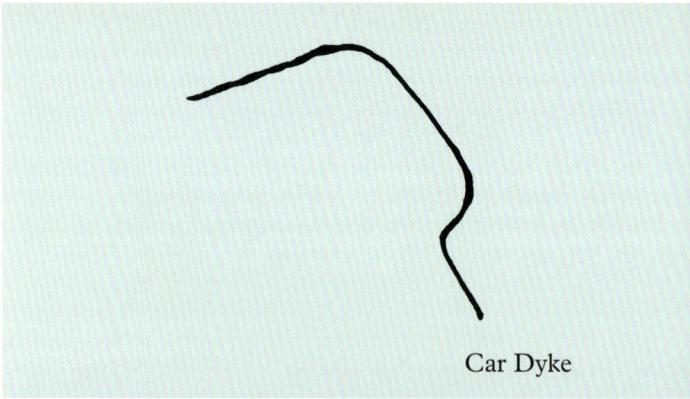

Car Dyke

Walk 15
on Car Dyke, Nocton
4 October 2007

artist unknown
Landscape with Buildings, Cows and Sheep

Recalled by Iain Sinclair

Iain Sinclair:

"…When you look at the tree, it's silhouetted, and it bifurcates – it is in fact two trees that have grown together. There's a male form on the right-hand trunk – somewhat more sturdy, somewhat direct. The left-hand trunk is slenderer, and leans away, forming a 'V', which is repeated throughout as the tree grows up, with continual bifurcation."

[…]

"The tree itself is rounded in its forms. It's almost like a cauliflower; it's like a parachute of leafage – very rich, very dense, above this slender tree trunk. And therefore, I think, slightly threatening, slightly standing in judgement against this pastoral scene, at twilight, in an otherwise reasonably anonymous landscape. Scrub woods on the horizon as if this tree has been nominated to stand for all the others, and to do something significant. And as I look at it, the branch forms beneath it begin to burn through the foliage, and the foliage folds back on itself."

[…]

"…I think I'd have to stay with the tree for a very long time to see how the tree becomes the hemispheres of a brain; the way the tree becomes an absence. The tree itself is simply that dark place where the world doesn't come. The tree is itself and nothing else, and the act of observing it becomes finally redundant."

[…]

"But we're a looking at this painting in a particular way. It could be left as a fairly recessive image that you might pass by in an art gallery, but challenged

to stop and be part of that painting, to engage with that painting, brings the focus entirely on something that's probably out of balance with the artist's intention, which is the tree; the tree becomes everything."

"And in this context, the tree becomes the world. The tree becomes a human identity. The tree becomes the splitting of the human brain. The tree becomes a kind of marriage between male and female, and the tree becomes something that will be judged."

"And then all that falls away and you've simply got this arrangement of space and form – that the roundness is there, it puffs and it billows; it's knobbly, the leaf forms become a solidity. And hanging low, off the bare branches at the bottom, are like two faint spectral hanged figures, just excrescences that drop away from the tree, slightly sinister, slightly strange, but avoiding drama, and avoiding rhetoric and simply staring kind of mutely back, in a very calm sort of way, at the person who is coming to look at it, and is coming to come to terms with it, and talk about those arrangements of energy and shape and form and structure and colour. All of which happened a long time ago. All of which depicts somewhere, which isn't there. And all of which is now recalled in a landscape that has no direct connection with it, is just a kind of absence. But in which the clouds hang, slivered, cirrus clouds, at the end of a particular day; another day, at which we recall the end of the first day. And in that relation is still some kind of dramatic exchange."

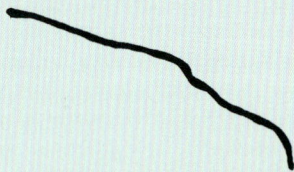

Butterwick Low

Walk 16

on Butterwick Low, Boston
5 October 2007

Alfred George Webster (1852–1916)
Mr Bland's Orchard, Heighington, Lincoln

Recalled by Sharon Morris

Sharon Morris:

"I'm trying to remember the painting that I saw a couple of hours ago. I can see an orchard, pink blossom, four dominant trees. The one on the left-hand side is the nearest, then comes the one on the right-hand side, then another one on the left, and a further one on the right. They're mainly pink blossom, like cherry trees, but I think they must be apple trees. The one on the left has a slightly orange hue of pink and the one on the right is extremely dusty, a sort of dusky bluey pink. And the two left ones merge together, and the one on the right, which is growing out of the frame, stands in front of one with white blossom; and then beyond that, a further orchard of pink blossom where everything merges together."

"And those four trees are in a field. They all fork at the top of the trunk towards the left, as if bent by prevailing wind, or as if the light draws them to the left. The left-hand one sort of blocked by the top of the frame, whereas the right-hand one grows way beyond the frame. Must be the tallest tree in that field…"

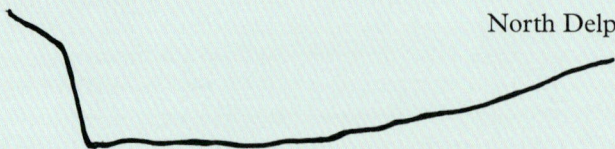

Greetwell Hall

North Delph

Walk 17
Greetwell Hall to North Delph
18 **October** 2007

Robert Noble (1857–1917)
On The Dean, East Linton

Recalled by Susanna Paisley

Susanna Paisley:

"…Around the central boulder there's a ring or an encircling of light, frothy willow, maybe weeping willows, which are those lovely pale, grey, silvery colours, and then there's other sorts of trees, maybe something like twenty trees in all, and at the centre of the painting, above the large boulder, there's maybe some kind of broad-leaved tree, or maybe it's a conifer, and then directly above and slightly to the right of that there's blue sky. But in terms of the trees, round to the right-hand side of the painting, there's a tall maybe broad-leaved tree, so they are darker colours – although there is one bright blotch of the willow leaves illuminated by the sun, which stands out against those darker colours… Another memory I have of the painting is there's a little…looks like maybe a kind of a spindly little conifer of some kind, maybe a fir tree or something, which is very feeble, and it's leaning over into the boulder, sort of resting its head on the boulder in a way… and there are some branches that drip down into the water very gently. And they slightly move, to the left, to the east, with that wind that's moving them."

Dunholme

79

Sch

Sewage
Works

Honeyholes Lane

Waltham
House

Dunholme
Lodge

29

Garage

Lincoln Road

78

Dunholme
Holt

Scothern Cliff
Farmhouse

Heath Road

The Granary

Scothern Beck

32

Nettleham
Heath Farm

77

Quarry
(dis)

Skelton
House
Farm

Nettleham Road

29

Nettleham
Heath

28

Heath
Farm

27

Nettleham Beck

NETTLEHAM CP

31

76

Sewage
Works

Richmond
Farm

Police
HQ

Nettleham

75

Bishop's
Manor
(site of)

Lodge
Farm

ROMAN ROAD

Greetwell Lane
Farm

Greetwell Lane

74

North
Greetwell

Wrassby Road East

28

Westfield Lane (Track)

Westfield
Farm

Ramper

DUNHOLME CP

Pickerings Meadow
Nature Reserve

Ashing Lane (Track)

Ashlin
Farm

Scothern North Drain

SCOTHERN CP

Stainton Lane

13

Manor
House

Red Barn
Farm

Hedgerow Farm

Scothern

Sch

TN
Gro

Langworth

Cemy

13

Cro

19

Oil Depot

Hall
Farm

Depot

New Ten
Acre Covert

SUDBROOKE CP

Manor
Farm

Sudbrooke
Park

Sudbrooke

Hall
Farm

South
Moor

Hatchery

13

Barfield
House

A158

14

Barfield Lane
Farm

19

Barfields
Farm

North Lane (Track)

Oil Gathering
Centre

Sewage
Works

REEPHAM CP

Reepham

or
m

14

14

Cemy

Dairy
Farm

Reepham

Sebald Memorial Walk
14 December 2006

Recalled by Simon Pope, accompanied by
Nicholas Thornton, then Curator of Art at
Norwich Castle Museum & Art Gallery

(Wind interference)
…(inaudible)…

Simon Pope: "…the trees in the photographic image are very, appear very tall and slender and we see the really high contrast against a grey, flat sky. The trees have obviously been damaged in some way, they look like they've been pushed over and we take it that there's been some kind of, it doesn't look like they've been cut down; the way they've collapsed it looks like there's been some force that's knocked them over. The tallest of the trees, maybe – actually the tree that's closest to us, has collapsed and fallen to the right of the, of the image and it's pushing, it's kind of falling towards the top right-hand side of the image, almost out of the frame. It has, it still has leaves and branches; it looks like a coniferous tree of some kind, like a fir tree of some kind – quite soft foliage on it, it takes our eye up to the top right-hand side of the frame. And then, immediately below that, right at the foot of the frame, is a very… very straight but relatively small and slender… tree trunk maybe, which is picked out in very, in almost white around it and it really struck me that there's a kind of glow around several of these trees that are depicted. At the foot of the frame there are trees that aren't damaged, that appear to be in the far distance; they kind of run in a continuous line across the foot of the image. On the left-hand side the trees are destroyed to a greater extent – it looks like they're, from

and ash in no time. Not far from Orford, and already tired from my long walk, this notion took possession of me when I was hit by a sandstorm. I was approaching the eastern fringe of Rendlesham Forest, which covers several square miles and was for the most part reduced to broken and splintered timber in the terrible hurricane of the 16th of October 1987. Suddenly, in the space of a few minutes, the bright sky darkened and a wind came up,

the dust across the arid land in sinister spirals. The remnants of daylight were being extinguished an

... after the great hurricane. As darkness closed in from ... on like a noose being tightened, I tried in vain to ... through the swirling and ever denser obscurement, ... that a short while ago still stood out clearly, but ... passing moment the space around became more ... Even in my immediate vicinity I could soon not ... guish any line or shape at all. The mealy dust streamed ... left to right, from right to left, to and fro on every side, ... on high and powdering down, nothing but a dancing ... whirl for what must have been an hour, while further ... and, as I later learnt, a heavy thunderstorm had broken. When ... he worst was over, the wavy drifts of sand that had buried the ... broken timber emerged from the gloom. Gasping for breath, ... my mouth and throat dry, I crawled out of the hollow that ... had formed around me like the last survivor of a caravan that had ... come to grief in the desert. A deathly silence prevailed. Ther ... was not a breath, not a birdsong to be heard, not a rustl ... nothing. And although it now grew lighter once more, the s ... which was at its zenith, remained hidden behind the ba ... of pollen-fine dust that hung for a long time in the air. ... I thought, will be what is left after the earth has groun ... down. – I walked the rest of the way in a daze. All I re ... is that my tongue was stuck to the roof of my mouth a ... felt as if I were walking on the spot. When at las ... Orford, I climbed to the top of the castle keep, from ...

what I recall, some of them are completely broken
in two, some of them have snapped. The top half,
the top parts of the trees have collapsed down.
And there are maybe six, I think, or more of these
trees in the foreground that are our, that become
our, focus in the image. They're all equally dense
and black. Some of the shapes they form are
quite complex; on the left-hand side of the frame
there are many branches and many leaves and
they're too complex for me to describe in detail
their sort of relationships and shapes; the shapes
they make. Most of the frame, the background is
a grey, it's, there's some kind of diagonal line
across it, it's obviously clouds and there are
patterns formed by the clouds and they kind of
slope away to the bottom right of the frame and
something I've really noticed as well is the photocopy, it's a photocopy… (inaudible)… it's a very
kind of low-quality image that we're trying to, that
we're looking at and there are kind of some very
thin white banding on the surface of the image.
But most of our focus is on the trees that have
been damaged beyond, beyond our kind of
usual, beyond our expectation, I suppose; it's
hard to imagine trees being damaged in that way
unless they're purposefully being cut down.

Nicholas Thornton: Trying to recollect the image,
it seems like the image is almost dominated by
the sky, the clouds seem to be quite broken up
and there seems to be sunlight shining through
them, it seems like it's perhaps in the early
morning or maybe in, late in the evening and the
sun's quite low in the sky and then against this
cloud-like background, there seems to be a line
of trees in the foreground and they're sort of
silhouetted against this grey sky and the clouds
and I think in the foreground there's six prominent
trees, I remember six prominent trees, four in a

kind of group on the left-hand side of the photograph and then two towards the right-hand side
of the photograph and they kind of create a kind
of 'V' shape; the largest tree is collapsed against
the tree on the extreme right in a way in this
foreground part of the photograph so it creates
a kind of upside down 'V' shape and the tree that
seems to have fallen against the other tree kind
of moves right up to the top right-hand side and
that tree retains most of its leaves whereas most
of the leaves in the other trees have been completely destroyed and it seems like the image is
the result of maybe a storm or wind damage in
some way. The foreground as I say is dominated
by the six trees but then when you look to the
background of the photograph, back of the image,
there seems to be a line of trees that perhaps
border the edge of a forest or perhaps a wind-
break on the edge of a field and those trees they
are the same kind of trees – they're conifers as
well – and they've retained most of their leaves
aswell and don't seem to be so damaged so the
real destruction is in the foreground of the image.
The four trees towards the left of the image have
all been snapped off completely and you can
barely recognise what they're like, there's a complex kind of web of branches and overlapping
branches there on the left and then over to the
right of the image there's another very narrow,
straight tree that's is almost not recognisable as
a tree and it could even be a telegraph pole and
then at the very foreground there's not very much
kind of vegetation or foliage, you can't see much
at all but at the very bottom there's perhaps some
damaged stumps and one of them forms a kind
of almost like a triangle shape and it could almost
be a spire of a church in the distance. So the
over… kind of overall picture really is one of
damage and destruction… (inaudible)…

Biographies

Rex Hancy is the author of *Notable Trees of Norwich*, and has been East Anglian Regional Co-ordinator of the British Plant Gall Society since its founding in 1985. His guide, *The Study of Plant Galls in Norfolk*, was published in 2001 by the Norfolk and Norwich Naturalists' Society.

George Szirtes' poems began appearing in national magazines in 1973 and his first book, *The Slant Door*, was published in 1979. It won the Faber Memorial Prize the following year. Szirtes won the 2004 T. S. Eliot Prize, for his collection *Reel*.

Marjorie Allthorpe-Guyton is a writer, and former Director of Visual Arts, Arts Council England and Editor of Artscribe International. She co-authored with Dr Miklos Rajnai catalogues of works by John Sell Cotman in the collection of Norwich Castle Museum, whilst working as Assistant Keeper at the museum.

Amanda Hopkinson is Director of The British Centre for Literary Translation, (founded by W.G. Sebald) near South Walsham Broad, Norfolk. She is the Chair of the Writers in Translation Committee of English PEN.

Tom McCarthy is an artist and novelist. He is the author of *Remainder* and *Men in Space*. McCarthy's ongoing art project, the International Necronautical Society, is a semi-fictitious avant-garde network that surfaces through publications, proclamations, denunciations and live events.

Hari Kunzru is a novelist and journalist and author. He won a Betty Trask Award and the Somerset Maugham Award for *The Impressionist*. His second novel, *Transmission*, was published in the summer of 2004 and was named one of the *New York Times*' notable books of the year. In 2005 he published the short story collection *Noise* and in August 2007 Penguin Hamish Hamilton published *My Revolutions*.

Nicci Gerrard and **Sean French** began work on their first joint novel in 1995 and adopted the pseudonym of Nicci French. *The Memory Game* was published to great acclaim in 1997 followed by *The Safe House* (1998), *Killing Me Softly* (1999), *Beneath the Skin* (2000), *The Red Room* (2001), *Land of the Living* (2002), *Secret Smile* (2003), *Catch Me When I Fall* (2005) and *Losing You* (2006). Their latest novel together is *Until It's Over* (2007).

Brian Dillon is a writer and critic. He has contributed to *Cabinet*, *The London Review of Books*, *The New Statesman*, *Modern Painters*, *Art Review* and *The Wire*. His first book, *In the Dark Room*, won the Irish Book Awards non-fiction prize, 2006.

Ken Worpole is a writer on architecture, landscape and urban social policy issues. His work concerns the quality of contemporary urban life, and he has worked with the think-tanks Comedia and Demos on new forms of civil society: notably on the planning and design of urban landscapes, the renewal of public institutions – parks, public libraries, hospices and cemeteries – as well as the pleasures of life in the open air.

Trezza Azzopardi is a novelist. Her first work, *The Hiding Place*, was shortlisted for the Booker Prize and the James Tait Black Memorial Prize, and won the Geoffrey Faber Memorial Prize. *Remember Me*, published in 2004, was shortlisted for the Arts Council Wales Book of the Year. Her latest novel, *Winterton Blue*, explores her self-confessed obsession with memory and forgetting.

Geoff Dyer has written several acclaimed novels and non-fiction works, including *But Beautiful, Yoga For People Who Can't Be Bothered To Do It* and, most recently, *The Ongoing Moment*. Awards for his books include the Somerset Maugham Prize, and a place as finalist in the National Book Critics Circle.

Sally O'Reilly is a writer and critic on contemporary art. With interests spanning philosophy, science and politcs, she has contributed to *Art Monthly, Frieze, Contemporary, Modern Painters, Time Out*, alongside numerous contemporary arts exhibition catalogues.

Stuart Jeffries is a journalist. Since 1990, he has worked for *The Guardian* as a TV critic, Friday Review editor, Paris correspondent, columnist and feature writer.

David Matless is Professor of Cultural Geography at the University of Nottingham. He is the author of *Landscape and Englishness*, and has published extensively on the cultural landscapes of East Anglia.

Iain Sinclair's novels include *Downriver, Radon Daughters*, and *Dining on Stones* (which was shortlisted for the Ondaatje Prize). His recent titles include *London, City of Disappearances* and *Edge of the Orison.*

Sharon Morris is an artist and a poet who teaches at the Slade School of Fine Art. Her collection, *False Spring*, was published by Enitharmon, 2007. She has exhibited photography, film and video, and performed live artworks bringing together spoken text and projected images.

Dr Susanna Paisley is a conservation biologist, who has lived and worked across Latin America. She now lives in London and works with a variety of environmental groups and universities. In 1997, she was awarded the Whitley Award.

Simon Pope is an artist and Reader in Fine Art at Cardiff School of Art & Design. His recent work investigates the conventions of walking and landscape – walking with others, entering into dialogue to construct representations of landscape. Other work includes *Painting from Memory* (2008), *London Bridge Recall* (2007) and *Gallery Space Recall* (2006).

Pope represented Wales at the Venice Biennale of Fine Art, 2003. His research project Walking Together is a study of the modes of sociality and walking in contemporary art practice, supported by Transmedia, Brussels.

The Memorial Walks
Simon Pope

Published by Film and Video Umbrella
© 2008, Film and Video Umbrella, the artist
and the authors
Edited by Steven Bode and Nina Ernst
Designed by Herman Lelie
Produced by fandg.co.uk
Funded by Arts Council England
With additional support from: Transmedia,
Brussels, Centre for Fine Art Research at
Cardiff School of Art & Design and Katholieke
Universiteit Leuven

ISBN: 978-1-904270-26-3

Photography (walks) © Simon Pope,
Brada Barassi and Bevis Bowden
Photography (paintings) © Mike Harrington
and Bevis Bowden

Sound recordings: Ross Adams, Brada Barassi
and Bevis Bowden

Thanks to: Nicholas Thornton at Norwich
Castle Museum and Art Gallery, Jill Sullivan,
Andrea Martin and Julie Bush at The Collection,
Lincoln, Jeremy Millar, Philip Cowell, Stefania
Bonelli, Caroline Smith, Beki Pope and
Steven Devleminck

Special thanks to all the writers/walkers

To hear the writers' recollections in full:
go to www. waterlog.fvu.co.uk

Film and Video Umbrella
8 Vine Yard, London SE1 1QL
Tel 020 7407 7755
Fax 020 7407 7766
Email info@fvu.co.uk

film and video umbrella   ARTS COUNCIL ENGLAND   Transmedia   {cfar centre for fine art research